Under
The Moon.

Dean Ryan

deanryanpoetry.com

@deanryanpoetry

ISBN :

Under
The Moon.

Dean Ryan

Dedicated to

when the moon and stars were aligned.

Contents

Broken.

different.

she was a rose,
in a field of daisies.
unique and beautiful,
a color my eyes had not seen before,
i loved to watch her bloom.

sorry.

i want to hold you in the night,
until the sun shines bright.
kiss you on your lips,
while my personality flips.
why are you still here?
you didn't disappear.

i take you to the lake,
apologize for my biggest mistake.
tell you i'm sorry,
you say not to worry.

i was scared of what you'd find,
when you walked into my mind.
you know exactly what's inside,
it's been a wild ride.

i never meant to upset you,
those hurtful words are untrue.
filled with more than one emotion,
our love is one complex potion.

dive under the blue,
i could swim forever with you.
we wait for the first star,
i'm happy we made it this far.

home.

i'm coming home to you,
but didn't have a clue.
you locked the door,
and didn't love me anymore.
how could this be so?
i couldn't let you go.

game over.

playing with your heart,
from the start.
just like a video game,
every day was the same.
with my controller,
you became emotionally bipolar.
using my fingers to manipulate,
i determined our fate.
into the wrong direction i drove her,
and suddenly we became game over.

last dance.

where is your heart tonight?
why did we have to fight?
am i inside your mind?
was i truly left behind?
i gave you everything i had,
are you even sad?

helpless while you tear me apart,
wish we could go back to the start.
i would change my ways,
make it feel like those early days.

wide awake in the night,
our memories are the only light.
pain in my veins,
how did it all go up in flames?

i look to the moon and stare,
glorious misery fills the air.
i wanted another chance,
but you said this was our last dance.

dreaming of you.

in a lonely town,
with the dark after sundown.
i sit by my window,
i hear leaves blow.
listening to the rain,
but it can't wash away my pain.

so i gaze upon a star,
and wonder where you are.

close my eyes,
and see those pretty skies.
on a summer night,
when i held you tight.

on a cliff by the sea,
with you, i felt so free.
staring out into the blue,
i knew that love is true.

wake up in the dark,
thunder and lightning spark.
i listen to my heart,
it's been you from the start.

in my room.

i'm back again,
in the place that feels like home.
nobody around,
not even a sound.
just the breeze,
blowing in the trees.
it makes me feel free,
and i can just be me.

in my room,
i cry.
i die.
i weep.
i sleep.

but it's all just for you,
because nothing else is true.

my heart is buried in a tomb,
but the flowers still bloom.
in the dead of night,
when we lose our sight.

dreaming of the sun,
while we're still young.

i remember your smile,
and it's been a while.

so i just stay in my room,
and think of you.

come back soon,
and lets gaze at the moon.

blue.

dancing under stormy skies.
laughing while the cars pass me by.
i want you to know,
since i let you go,
i feel blue.

take me on a wild ride,
lead me to the other side.
teach me all that you know,
i've been waiting to go,
somewhere new.

and you still swim the sea,
under crashing waves you're free.
come up for air,
our eyes meet in a stare.
in the pouring rain,
your lips kiss away my pain.

the end of the world.

when the world stops turning,
and the trees are burning,
when the rivers stop flowing,
and the wind stops blowing.

meet me by the sea,
you know where i'll be.
our feet buried in the sand,
i'll hold your hand.

your smile makes me fly,
now we're in the sky,
nothing below matters,
we watch as the earth shatters.

garden of a broken heart.

watching you sprout from the earth,
i never understood your worth.
until you vanished from my garden,
i begged for your pardon.
rain starts to pour,
i long for your touch once more.
collapsing in the soil,
covered in black turmoil.
the sky will never be blue,
nothing compares to you.

don't go.

a glimmer of hope,
to help me cope.
i can't accept the fact,
that you broke the pact.
even when you say,
you don't want to stay.
i don't want to grieve,
so my mind won't believe,
that you would really leave.

tears of love.

when you walked out,
everything changed,
i could feel it in my veins,
leaving me in the worst way,
i begged you not to,
but you broke me anyway.

ashamed.

after all these years,
save your crocodile tears.
it should have been face to face,
the way you left a disgrace.
over the phone,
your heart turned to stone.
i don't know you anymore,
disregarding everything we once swore.
ashamed i gave you my heart,
so you could tear it apart.

why.

when you said goodbye,
it made me want to die.
all i could do is cry,
it felt like a lie.

the truth.

if i let you inside,
i could no longer hide,
i'm scared of what you'll find,
if you wandered through my mind.

stay.

i look into your eyes,
to see what you disguise.

the games you play,
lead me astray.

nothing seems clear,
except my biggest fear.

your heart went away,
when i needed you to stay.

goodbye.

my eyes need to see you cry,
my ears need to hear you lie,
my body needs to purify,
my soul needs to fly,
my heart needs to say goodbye.

dead.

today my mind is dead.
can't get the words out of my head,
thinking about everything you said.

i belong to you.

when the moon rises,
over the dark sea,
the mountain makes me think of you.

memories dance in my brain,
as i drive these winding roads.
i look to the sky,
as life passes me by.

spark.

i protected you from the rain,
shielded you from the pain.
even when we were apart,
i felt you in my heart.
out of nowhere,
you stopped to care.
said you lost the spark,
then left me in the dark.

the devil is blonde.

you said i was a keeper,
our love was so much deeper.
freckled devil on your shoulder,
i wonder what you told her.
she plays you like a guitar,
put an end to us from a far.
she was jealous of our connection,
it became her obsession.
together we were the perfect percussion.
this was not her first attempt at destruction.

angel dust.

i've never been high,
but you fly me to the sky.
swim into my vein,
take away the pain.
my vision was clouded by your dust,
the only angel i trust.
the edge of a blade kisses my wrist,
breaking these walls with my fist.
one hit from you and i'm paralyzed,
laying on the floor my heart capsized.
breathing you in is my sin,
your lips taste sweet like heroin.

our song.

if you give me another chance,
like fire we will dance.
under a glowing moon,
to the melodies of that perfect tune.
until the sky turns light blue,
i will slowly fade into you.

betrayal.

you told me it was ride or die.
when you left me,
you didn't even cry.
your last words were strong,
so hurtful and so wrong.
over the phone was your final goodbye,
you basically told me to go die.

first love.

into the wild fire,
i've never fallen from higher.
when you started to turn,
my world started to burn,
i tried to take cover,
you were my first lover.

daydreaming.

at night i run to the sea,
the horizon is all i can see.
but in the back of my mind,
you're all i can find.
so i lay in the sand,
and reach out my hand.
close my eyes,
i feel butterflies.
until the morning sky turns blue,
i only want to be with you.

as she took flight.

i almost didn't notice,
it felt like hypnosis.
her claws digging into my heart,
her wings a work of art.
i was under her spell,
but it hurt like hell.

prayers in the dark.

i was the moon,
you were my star,
i made you who you are.

you left me in a heartless way,
but every night i still pray,
that you'll be okay.

Fury.

cancer.

you took away your voice,
left me no choice.
cut me out like cancer,
with no explanation or answer.

psychopath.

did you think i would break?
that was your biggest mistake.
after your attack,
i took the knife out of my back.
feel my wrath,
Baby, i'm a psychopath.

cheers.

inside your mind,
thought you would find.
me curled in a ball,
crying against the wall.
the truth is i'm more than fine,
so go drown in your cheap bottle of wine.

the pretender.

i look into your eyes,
and see through your lies.
you mastered the art of pretend,
when your heart wants it all to end.

revenge.

did you think i'd let you go free?
there's a fire burning inside me.
gasoline in my veins,
unleash me from these chains.
i want you to feel my storm,
watch as i transform.
pierce you with this sword,
your heart punctured, bloody and gored.
my lover turned into my betrayer,
so i became her slayer.

venom.

wipe away these tears,
of our lost years.
from these vengeful eyes,
you'll watch as i rise,
like a cobra,
in the dead of night,
you'll feel my bite.
poison dripping from my fangs,
dark blue like denim,
you're forever covered in my venom.

howling.

when the night sky was black,
i became a maniac.
howling at the moon,
creating a destructive monsoon.
it was something i couldn't control,
secretly trying to climb out of the hole,
i always tried to hide,
but you discovered my dark side.

Pain.

nocturnal.

i can't sleep anymore,
my heart is at war.
i feel so sad,
lost the best thing i had.
so i close my eyes,
dream of those purple skies.
when i loved you right,
all through the night.

never.

i had a dream about you,
but it'll never come true.
we were under that big palm tree,
your hands all over me.
our love felt so real,
an emotion i forgot i could feel.

moon & sun.

i showed her a place,
in the gloomiest part of space,
she had never seen anything,
quite so frightening,
she only knew of the light,
as she shined so bright,
she was the sun,
it made her want to run,
far away from me,
she never wanted to see,
but i hope she comes back soon,
to the dark side of the moon.

nobody.

our love is history,
why you left a mystery.
i'm scared to death,
it makes me lose my breath.
that you found someone new,
but there's nothing i can do.
it doesn't seem real,
that he could ever make you feel,
the connection we share,
nobody will ever compare.

withdrawal.

i feel sick without you tonight,
it doesn't feel right.
can't get you out my head,
wishing you were in my bed.
tears running down my face,
in this lonely place.
missing you is the worst withdrawal,
you were my greatest love of all.

ghost.

you became a ghost,
but i still miss you the most.
i hope that you'll return,
before i slowly burn.

space.

lost in space,
in a far away place.
where time means something,
and everything means nothing.
except for you and i,
searching for you in the black sky.

drifting away,
when you should have tried to stay.
the air is becoming more dense,
nothing about this makes sense.
losing my air supply,
i spend my last moments wondering why,
you said goodbye.

crutch.

crying for you,
only because the sky is blue.
but looking deep inside,
i can no longer hide.
it was never supposed to be
forever you and me.

i couldn't give you more,
because you're not what i'm looking for.
you were never my wife,
you just came into my life,
on the darkest night,
when i needed to be held tight.

i'm sad to see you go,
and even though
i'll miss your gentle touch,
you were honestly just my crutch.

galaxy.

once you left my sight,
we became strangers overnight.
trapped in a black hole,
after i gave you my soul.
somewhere far away,
no words left to say.
lost in time and space,
in this silent place.
my world overcome with madness,
i am consumed by sadness.
a force stronger than gravity,
in this lonely galaxy.

vultures.

sitting in the shadows,
my loneliness grows.
without you next to me,
i'm drowning in the black sea.
gasping for air,
but you don't even care.
the waves bring me to shore,
but i can't take it anymore.
vultures circling overhead,
my soul slowly becomes dead.

surrender.

i need to get off of this roller coaster ride,
you're intentionally trying to hurt me inside.
playing with my heart and soul,
is my destruction your ultimate goal?
fighting back the tears,
i'm thinking back to all our years.
you've hurt me many times,
you committed unforgivable crimes.

but i kept letting you back in,
this was my greatest sin.
i was so blind from the start,
you don't deserve my beautiful heart.
took our photographs out of the drawer,
ripping them, i watch them fall to the floor.

her own actions will end her,
but in this moment i surrender.
this is not a war worth dying for,
i can't take your games anymore.

more.

when i started to think,
my heart started to sink.
i started to realize,
we were built on lies.
when you opened your gate to a stranger,
i should have recognized the danger.
but i let you back into my arms,
hypnotized you with my charms.
if you hurt me once before,
i should have shut the door,
but i still wanted more.

antibiotic.

rising above,
i realized true love
is extremely rare,
like a perfect flare,
from a shooting star,
somewhere high and far.
two minds must connect,
but our chemistry had a defect,
my creative antibiotic,
could not cure your robotic.

someone else.

feeling fragile, but strong,
i smiled, but it felt wrong.
she was someone new,
but i still feel blue.
her words are neglected,
because my mind is disconnected.
i couldn't look her in the eye,
being there felt like a lie.
we laughed and we spoke,
but my heart is still broke.
i couldn't compel myself,
i wanted her to be someone else.

sun.

standing on the lonely shores,
her eyes are not yours,
i want to be with you,
floating in the deep blue,
i don't want just anyone,
you were my sun,
on my darkest day,
all you had to do was stay.

crave.

can you see me burning?
can you feel my hurting?
the silence is piercing me,
the night wants to break me.
going crazy talking to myself,
your photograph no longer on my shelf.
i scream to the sky,
on my knees wondering why.
you put my heart into a grave,
trying my best to be brave,
in this cold and lonely cave,
when it's your touch i crave.

always.

i know you still cry,
while you live a lie.
you're not fine,
part of your heart is still mine.
you can't erase my name,
our memories will always remain.

echoes in the rain.

looking into the dark sky,
i listen to the moon sigh,
black crows flying overhead,
all the flowers are dead,
there's a black thorn tree,
lingering above me,
casting a shadow of blame,
i hear your name,
echoing in the rain,
it still brings me pain.

abyss.

how will i get through this,
i'm falling into a dark abyss.
without you by my side,
i can no longer hide.
when people ask about us,
i can't find the strength to discuss.

emotional.

even when i'm alone,
in the dark on my own.
i feel your existence,
my emotions hold no consistence.

rivers of pain.

now that you're gone,
from dusk till dawn,
memories dance in my brain,
while these rivers of pain,
run through my vein,
since we've been apart,
straight into my broken heart.

winter.

struck by lightning,
losing you was frightening.
the sounds of thunder,
makes me wonder.
what's on your mind,
what would i find.
even after you decided to turn,
this fire continues to burn.
i can't erase you out of my mind,
my heart is of a different kind.
under my skin like a splinter,
you became the coldest winter.
without any reasons,
you changed like the seasons.

cocoon.

i feel like i'm going to die,
when a butterfly,
flying in the sky,
passes me by.
while i cry,
under the full moon,
near the lagoon,
trapped in this dark cocoon,
hoping to break free soon.

dead to you.

and i still wanted it to be,
just you and me.
Baby, can't you see,
i miss you terribly.
how could it be true,
after all that we've been through.
you don't have a clue,
of all the things i'd do,
for us to just be two.
but i never really knew,
that i could be dead to you.

Memories.

first kiss.

once we start,
lightning strikes the heart.
kissing my lips in the dark,
igniting a spark.
and a flame begins to burn,
as the world continues to turn.
like a beautiful silhouette in the sun,
our body's become one.

holiday.

i'm the hunter,
you're my prey,
standing in the doorway,
your naked body on display,
ready to give it all away,
i watch as you obey,
all the words i say,
on that midsummer day,
i became your holiday.

my girl.

denim jacket with nothing underneath,
your heart was mine to keep.
snuck me in through your front door,
tip toes on your creaking floor.
put your hair behind you ear,
whispers only you could hear.
the butterflies inside you begin to whirl,
on the night i called you my girl.

my protector.

my heart was pounding,
like an alarm sounding.
i was ready to fall,
but you were my wall.
protecting me from pain,
when i was going insane.

drowning.

no matter how hard i swam,
i couldn't break free.
you were the strongest current in the sea,
and you consumed me.

by the sea.

you in that little red blouse,
in our small yellow house.
i want to give you more,
not just the things i swore.
my lonely heart breaks,
regretting my mistakes.
come back to me,
so we can live by the sea.

three turtles.

a black swan in the pond,
our unbreakable bond.
with you i feel so free,
on top of a cliff above the sea.
i jump into the endless blue,
i would do anything for you.
my feelings continue to grow,
as the current continues to flow.
a rainbow breaks through the sky,
i am so lucky to be your guy.
three sea turtles down below,
shining like rose gold begin to glow.
i see you on the shore,
i couldn't love you more.

everything.

turn the lights down low,
i watch the moon glow,
on your hips as they sway,
keep moving that way.

stay right where you are,
take my mind somewhere far,
turn you over slowly,
together we are no longer holy.

as our bodies intertwine,
i touch your beautifully curved spine,
in that moment i take control,
giving you everything inside my soul.

storm.

in the front of my car,
you're my star.
the music plays,
i'm falling into a magical daze,
watching you feel the beat,
i pull you onto my seat.
we start to groove,
i love how you move.
our eyes meet,
on this dark street.
keeping each other warm,
together we are the perfect storm.

Hope.

angel.

i look to the moon,
i hope to see you soon.
i miss hearing your voice,
i wish i had a choice,
to go back to any day,
just so i could say,
i love you like no other,
our bond unlike any other.

another day passes by,
all i can do is cry.
i wish you were by my side,
my emotions can no longer hide.
the pain i felt when you said farewell,
it was the hardest i ever fell.

i feel you pass me by,
like an angel in the sky.
spread your wings and soar,
without you my hearts at war.
but i feel your essence,
it's the most powerful presence.

i close my eyes and there you are,
sitting on the brightest star.
i miss you more than words can say,
but i know that there will come a day.
when we fly together so free,
reunited for all of eternity.

wonderland.

tears on my face,
our memories lost in space.
my soul torn apart,
your cold heart,
took a piece of me,
when you set yourself free.
but one day you'll understand,
i was your wonderland.

when you were leaving,
i was disbelieving.
your actions were so deceiving,
now you're grieving.

one day you'll realize,
abandoning me wasn't wise.
shot yourself in the heart,
wishing you could go back to the start.
your mind filled with regret,
i was Romeo and you my Juliet.

i told you i would die for you,
did these words pass right through?
memories flood your mind,
of when the moon and stars were aligned.

a greek god above you,
my naked body like a statue.
i treated you like my wife,
i gave you so much of my life.
even though i feel betrayed,
since your feelings decayed.
i still feel it inside my chest,
my love, i wish you only the best.

better.

climb out of the hole,
forget about how much time they stole.
take your broken heart,
let all of those memories depart.
this is your new beginning,
soon you will be winning.
at the start things will be hard,
believing you're shattered and scarred.
holding on to a past,
that wasn't meant to last.

sleepless in the night,
thinking you just might,
break into a million pieces.
as your depression and anxiety releases,
into the dark air,
but out of your window you notice a golden glare.
catching your eye is the moonlight,
reminding you to win this fight.
because you are strong,
and losing you in this world would be so wrong.
as time passes you won't recall,
those lonely nights when you would bawl.

it will feel like a past life left behind,
long ago when you were blind.
one day walking by the sea,
you'll feel so free.
as you turn the corner,
you see another mourner.
you'll reach out your hand,
sit down together in the sand.
tell them your story,
how we are all destined for glory.
you look up to the sky,
a shooting star passes you by.
as if the universe sent you a letter,
saying you deserve so much better.

fairytale.

the hurt won't go away,
tomorrow is a new day,
i'll rise like the sun,
my new story has just begun,
so i close our final chapter,
although it was not happily ever after.

black beauty.

a long journey of fate,
my lady will wait.
as i ride through the night,
i become her dark knight.
upon this blazing stallion,
wearing my gold medallion.
i call her black beauty as she glides,
with her long graceful strides.
through endless fields of flowers,
during these long lonesome hours.
i dream of a place,
where i encounter her beautiful face.
i use all my power,
as i find the tower.
that holds my true love inside,
it's been a long treacherous ride.
defeating many evils along the way,
climbing the tower to where she lay.
i wake her with a kiss,
igniting a magical bliss.

the sea.

the sea is a good thing,
it has no face or eyes,
but that does not matter to him or her,
because the sea has no fear,
for anything that's near.

deep.

like waves in the sea.
come back and crash into me.
i've learned from my mistakes,
my love, i'll do whatever it takes.
for one more chance,
our final dance.

let's make love in slow motion,
i'll meet you at the end of the ocean.
where the sun goes to sleep,
rediscovering a love so deep.
we can hide on the horizon line,
forever your heart will be mine.

fade.

waiting for your call,
felt like i was going to fall.
i couldn't stay,
so i went away.
somewhere only we know,
where i could take it slow.
as the days pass by,
my feelings become colors in the sky.
turning into a different shade,
into the sunset i watch them fade.

letting go.

i needed to be alone,
in a place i can call my own.
away from all the noise,
so i could regain my poise.
somewhere far away,
where the sky is no longer grey.
and the sun shines,
while birds fly in perfect lines.
by the calm ocean,
i'll put my dreams into motion.
laying under sunflowers,
in these fields for hours and hours.
finding the beauty within the rain,
i'm letting go of my pain.
discovering peace within my heart,
ready for my fresh start.

mankind.

regretfully declined,
my beautiful mind,
is of a different kind,
intricately designed,
unique and undefined,
it was mistakenly left behind,
when you were blind,
it's something you will not find,
as you wander through mankind.

free.

we will be alright,
just hold on tight.
i don't want you to cry,
when i say goodbye.

you deserve so much better,
hidden inside my last letter.
you'll be able to see,
i'm setting you free.

so i let you fly away,
when i wish you would stay.
i watch and cry,
as your wings meet the sky.

one thing.

there are so many little things,
i want to tell you.
but there's one that i wish you knew...

i still miss you.

thank you for breaking my heart and
inspiring me to turn my pain into art.

Dean

Made in the USA
Middletown, DE
24 November 2019